My Book of
Rocks
AND
Minerals

Author: Dr. Devin Dennie

Editor Olivia Stanford
Senior designer Katie Knutton
Designer Emma Hobson
Editorial assistant Kathleen Teece
Design assistant Bettina Myklebust Stovne
DTP designers Syed Mohammad Farhan,
Mohd Rizwan
Jacket co-ordinator Francesca Young
Jackets designers Katie Knutton, Amy Keast
Managing editor Laura Gilbert
Managing art editor Diane Peyton Jones
Pre-production producer Nadine King
Producer Isabell Schart
Art director Martin Wilson
Publisher Sarah Larter
Publishing director Sophie Mitchell

First published in Great Britain in 2017 by
Dorling Kindersley Limited
80 Strand, London WC2R 0RL

Copyright © 2017 Dorling Kindersley Limited
A Penguin Random House Company
10 9 8 7 6 5 4 3 2 1
001-298703-Jul/2017

A CIP catalogue record for this book is
available from the British Library.
ISBN: 978-0-2412-8306-6

Printed and bound in China.

A WORLD OF IDEAS:
SEE ALL THERE IS TO KNOW

www.dk.com

Contents

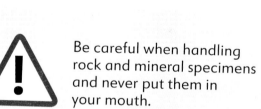

Be careful when handling rock and mineral specimens and never put them in your mouth.

Rock or mineral?

Minerals are the basic building blocks of rocks. Minerals themselves are made of different chemical "ingredients" and every one has a unique recipe. When mixtures of these minerals occur together we call them rocks.

A mineral is always made of crystal shapes. The crystals in this amethyst look like small pyramids.

MINERAL

Amethyst

How to tell them apart

Minerals have specific properties, such as colour and texture, that we can test to work out what they are. To identify a rock you have to look at all the minerals inside it and how they are combined.

You can clearly see that the rock gabbro contains a mix of white and black minerals.

Amethyst is a purple type of quartz. When quartz is colourless it is called "rock crystal".

Gabbro

ROCK

This gabbro is a "coarse-grained" rock because the mineral crystals inside it are large enough to see.

What is a gemstone?

A valuable piece of mineral is known as a gemstone. Its value depends on its rarity, colour, and how perfectly formed it is. Gemstones are often polished, or cut and put into jewellery.

A cut gemstone allows light to bounce around inside it, making the stone shimmer and sparkle!

Cut sapphire

Polished carnelian

Gemstones can be polished to make them shine using a rock tumbler.

Rockhounding

If you like to collect rocks and minerals, then you might be a rockhound! Rockhounding is the hobby of collecting rocks and minerals.

Rocks and minerals come in all colours of the rainbow.

Where to find gems

Rocks and minerals are everywhere, so it's easy to start a collection. You can go outside and start searching, or maybe go to a local rock and mineral show, or visit a rock shop. There might even be a local club you can join.

South Africa produces the highest value of minerals in the world.

Clubs or mineral shows

Joining a club or visiting a rock and mineral show is a great way to find out about collecting. You can discover all sorts of information, such as where you might find a certain rock type.

The Gem and Mineral Show in Tucson, Arizona, USA

Riverbeds and hillsides are great places to find minerals.

Out and about

The cheapest way to build your collection is to get out and collect yourself. On trips to the park or countryside keep your eyes to the ground – you never know what you may find!

Shops

Rock shops will often sell high-quality gems as well as small pieces of polished rocks and minerals. Keep an eye out for gems that might have been dyed different colours, such as the Dalmatian stones below.

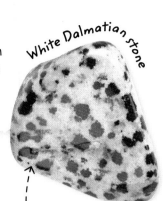
White Dalmatian stone

Agate

Spotty Dalmatian stone in its natural form is white.

Howlite is usually white with grey lines in it, but this one has been dyed blue.

Howlite

Rose quartz

Yellow Dalmatian stone

Sunstone

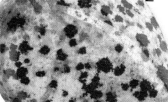
Blue Dalmatian stone

This Dalmatian stone has been dyed blue to make it more colourful.

Safety first!

Rocks and minerals are awesome, but you should be careful when handling them. Nothing here is really dangerous, but make sure you wash your hands after touching them and be aware of sharp edges.

Rhodochrosite

Wash your hands if you've touched: coal, shale, lapis lazuli, haematite, amazonite, galena, sodalite, malachite, chrysocolla, azurite, rhodonite, or rhodochrosite.

Be careful of sharp edges on: quartz, flint, dolomite, hornfels, obsidian, pyrite, tourmaline, and chalcedony.

Obsidian

Mica

Don't breathe in dust from: Pele's hair, pumice, amazonite, mica, or chalcedony, including tiger's eye.

Unearthing minerals

Rocks and minerals make up the ground beneath our feet, so we need to dig to get them out. Stone is often cut straight from the Earth in quarries, but sometimes tunnels called mines must be dug to find the right material.

Quarries like this provide exposed rock faces from which blocks of stone can be cut.

These marble blocks will be cut into smaller slabs or thin sheets.

Heavy equipment is needed to move the large stones and any leftover rock, called tailings.

Just one cubic metre of marble may weigh as much as 2,700 kg (6,000 lbs)!

Marble from this area in Italy has been used for thousands of years.

Big machines are used to slice up the strong marble into blocks.

Digging for treasure

Rocks and minerals are dug up for many reasons. Some rocks are useful as building materials, while minerals can contain metals such as iron or copper, which are used to create all sorts of objects. Other valuable minerals are unearthed to be sold as gemstones.

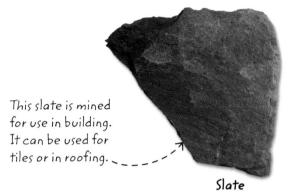

This slate is mined for use in building. It can be used for tiles or in roofing.

Slate

The mineral malachite is rich in the metal copper. Copper is often used to make electrical wires.

Malachite

Gemstones, such as rubies, are mined and then cut into different shapes for use in jewellery.

Ruby

Equipment

Rockhounds always head into the field with the proper equipment. These tools and supplies will keep you safe, and let you bring your finds back home in one piece!

Paintbrush

Brushes like these can be useful for removing dirt from finds.

Toothbrush

Toothpicks and chopsticks can be useful for scraping samples clean.

Maps

A map will help you get to where you are going. Just be sure to get permission first!

Toothpicks

Buckets are handy for many things: carrying your tools, sorting loose rocks, or taking your samples back home.

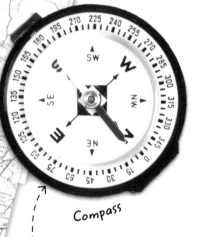

Compass

A compass will help you follow the map.

Bucket

An egg box makes a handy container for any delicate items you find while rockhounding. - - ⌄

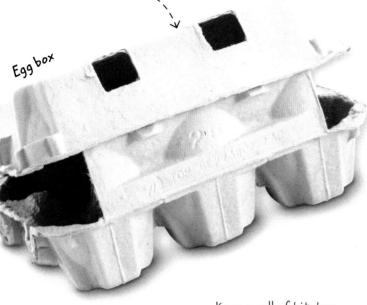

Egg box

Kitchen paper

Keep a roll of kitchen paper handy to wrap up your rocks and minerals for protection. ⌄

Staying safe

It is sensible to take supplies with you when you head out rockhounding. Make sure you pack what you need and always take an adult with you.

A backpack is useful for carrying your tools, supplies, and your rocks.

If it is sunny, don't forget your sunscreen, or if it looks cold, wear warm clothing.

Take water and a snack to keep your energy up.

It's good to wear a helmet if you are working where there are rocks overhead, in case any fall.

Kneepads can help make digging more comfortable.

Rock hunting

Collecting rocks and minerals is part detective work and part treasure hunt! Finding the right location and always getting permission to collect is the first step. Then all you need to do is start looking!

Watch out

It's important to stay safe when you're out rock collecting. Make sure you follow the steps below:

- Always take an adult with you
- Watch out for falling rocks when near cliffs or steep slopes
- Never enter mines or quarries
- Don't collect near roads
- Watch out for animals
- Don't move heavy rocks
- Watch out for the tide coming in at the seaside

Pick a location

Do some research before you go hunting, to know what you might find. You don't have to go far to discover interesting specimens – a garden or beach is ideal. Make sure you take an adult with you for safety!

You can find rocks in your garden, but you might have to dig to find them.

The motion of waves uncovers rocks, minerals, and fossils along the shoreline.

Small streams are great places to find tough minerals, such as quartz. Watch out for slippery rocks.

Cleaning

Specimens you collect often don't look perfect at first. You may need to scrub away the soil or clay around them. Soap and water, and a brush will help get rid of all the dirt.

Let any rocks you've washed dry out before you look at them, as they may appear a different colour.

Sponge and soapy water

Brush

Sometimes you will find a fossil or crystals stuck inside a rock. Use a magnifying glass to examine them.

Examining

Once your samples are clean, you can take a closer look at them. You may want to check your finds before you bring them home as rocks are heavy to haul around!

Creating a collection

A great way to enjoy rocks and minerals is to start your very own collection! You can display your favourite finds to show them to family and friends.

Museums can house hundreds of thousands of specimens.

At their best

Collections can include stones that are not only beautiful or rare, but that tell a story – perhaps from a memorable trip. There are lots of things you can do to keep your collection in top condition.

Some rocks have special properties, such as magnetism. Use a paperclip to amaze your friends with magnetic stones.

Minerals like halite need to stay dry. Packing cotton wool balls around them helps to absorb any moisture.

Some minerals may change colour when left in sunlight. You can store these sensitive stones in cloth bags to protect them.

You can create a display case for your collection from a carboard box and its lid.

A clear sheet of plastic makes a great viewing window.

Cotton wool balls placed inside each tube will help to prevent specimens moving around and breaking.

Cut up used paper towel rolls of different sizes to use as sample holders. If you need a wider tube you can cut two in half and glue them together.

What is a rock?

Making a rock is a bit like making a salad! Like salads, rocks are a mixture of different things – usually minerals, but also the remains of living things, such as shells. There are three types of rock, each made in a different way.

Igneous rocks are the most plentiful rocks on the Earth.

Igneous

Igneous rocks form when hot, molten magma, which comes from deep within the Earth, cools down. This often happens around volcanoes.

Ancient rocks

Some of the oldest known minerals on Earth are found in metamorphic rocks in Australia. These samples contain zircon (zer-con) crystals over 4.4 billion years old!

OLDEST ROCK

Granite

The minerals in granite "freeze" in place as magma cools.

Sedimentary

Sedimentary rocks are made when small pieces of other rocks, called sediments, are buried together. Sediments are made when water, wind, or ice break up existing rocks.

Limestone

— These fossils are the remains of animals' shells captured in the rock when it formed.

Metamorphic

Metamorphic rocks are made when other types of rock are melted and squeezed. They are squashed and heated until they form new rocks.

Marble

How are rocks made?

The inside of the Earth is made of many layers. Below the surface is a layer of rock so hot it has melted into a liquid – called magma. If this magma cools enough, or escapes to the surface, new rocks are made.

If you cut the Earth in half you would see its layers.

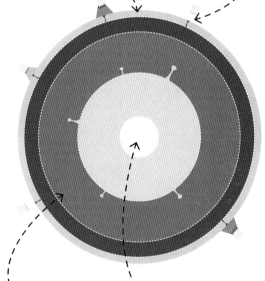

The outer layer of the Earth is called the crust. —

Volcanoes are holes in the Earth's surface where lava escapes.

The next two layers are the upper and lower mantle, made of hot rock. Magma is created at the top of the mantle.

The Earth's centre, or inner core, is solid metal. The outer core is liquid metal.

Marble is formed when limestone is squashed and heated.

Rock cycle

The rock cycle describes the life of every rock on Earth. During the rock cycle, rocks change from one type into another. You would have to wait around a long, long time to watch it happen. However, you can see how it works using wax crayons, which melt at much lower temperatures than rock!

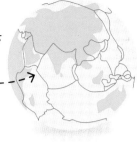

The surface layer of the Earth — the crust — is divided into pieces that fit together like a jigsaw puzzle.

Sedimentary crayon rock

By pressing layers of the crayon "sediments" together so they stick, you can see how a sedimentary rock is created.

Using a sharpener to break up crayons is similar to how the weather breaks up rocks into sediments.

Layers of rock are exposed as the stone is worn away.

Eroding

Water, wind, and ice weather and break up, or "erode", all rocks into tiny bits, called sediments. These sediments are washed away by rivers into the sea, where they build up in layers. Over time, the pressure of new layers makes the sediments stick together to make new sedimentary rocks.

The movement of the crust squeezes rocks and pushes up mountains.

Squeezing

The Earth's crust is divided into pieces, called plates. The plates move about, squeezing, stretching, and pulling the rocks between them. This creates fierce heat and pressure, which changes the rocks into metamorphic rocks.

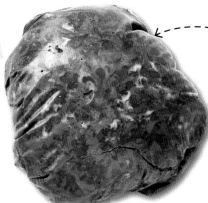

◄ – – – – – If the sedimentary crayon rock is warmed up and squeezed, the different colours start to run into each other, making a "metamorphic" crayon rock.

Metamorphic crayon rock

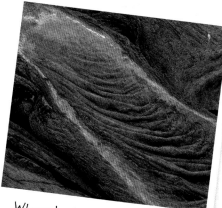
Where lava cools on the Earth's surface it makes new igneous rocks.

Melting

Rocks that are buried deeper, nearer the heat of the Earth's centre, can melt to form a hot liquid, called magma. If this magma escapes to the surface, it cools and turns into solid igneous rock.

Igneous crayon rock

◄ – – – If the wax melts completely, all the colours mix. If it is then left to cool, it forms a new "igneous" crayon rock.

Some varieties of granite are still waiting to finish their rock cycle after 4.2 billion years!

Granite

(GRAN-it)

Granite is a really tough rock! It forms when magma cools slowly, deep within the Earth, and it makes up most of the rock underneath the land. Granite is a popular stone used in road, rail, and building construction.

Granite contains light-coloured minerals such as feldspar, quartz, and mica.

Granite has crystals that are very easy to see.

Feldspar (FELD-spar)

Quartz (CWOR-ts)

Mica (MIKE-a)

Over time, granite breaks down to create much of the quartz sand on sandy beaches!

Monumental strength

Granite is ideal for making long-lasting sculptures. The heads of four American presidents are chiselled straight out of a granite cliff called Mount Rushmore, in South Dakota, USA.

Mount Rushmore

Obsidian

(ob-SID-ee-an)

Obsidian is a type of glass made by volcanoes! When volcanoes erupt explosively, magma meets air and water quickly, and "freezes" in place. It cools so fast that mineral crystals cannot form, so obsidian is not actually made of minerals, but it is a rock.

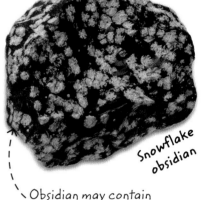

Snowflake obsidian

Obsidian may contain spots of white minerals. These are called "snowflakes".

Obsidian looks a bit like a curved conch shell when it breaks — a feature known as conchoidal fracturing.

Obsidian can have very sharp edges, so be careful when collecting it!

Obsidian gets its dark colour from small amounts of materials such as iron.

Basalt

(BA-salt)

Basalt is a volcanic rock that is made from runny, red-hot lava flows. It is a dark, tough, heavy rock that makes up much of the Earth's surface and ocean floor.

When magma that forms basalt cools more slowly, gabbro is formed instead.

Gabbro (GAB-roe)

MOST COMMON ROCK ON EARTH'S SURFACE

Bubbles of gas trapped in cooling lava create holes in the rock.

The crystals in basalt are too small to be seen, so the rock is all one colour.

Giant's Causeway

Six-sided

When basalt cools quickly, it often breaks into six-sided, or hexagonal, patterns. Famous places such as the Giant's Causeway in Northern Ireland or Devils Tower in Wyoming, USA, are examples of this.

Olympus Mons is a volcano made of basalt on the planet Mars. It is over 22 km (14 miles) high!

Unakite

(OON-a-KITE)

Unakite is formed from granite and is a semi-precious stone. It is a favourite of many collectors because of the unique green mineral it contains, called epidote (EP-ee-doh-t), and its colourful, speckled appearance.

Epidote

The green mineral epidote starts life as a type of white mineral called plagioclase (PLAY-jee-oh-clayze). Exposure to the weather changes the plagioclase from white to green.

The green patches are clumps of the mineral epidote. ------

The pink parts are crystals of the mineral orthoclase (OR-tho-clayze).

The name "unakite" comes from the discovery of the rock in the Unaka Mountains on the border of North Carolina and Tennessee, USA, where it is collected.

Pumice

(PUM-iss)

Have you ever seen foam on top of a fizzy drink? Pumice is nature's volcanic foam, and is one of the lightest rocks on Earth. It contains many small holes that were made by bubbles inside molten, liquid, volcanic glass as it erupted from a very gassy volcano.

The Ancient Romans used pumice to make concrete, so they could build tall buildings like the Colosseum.

Pumice is made up of volcanic glass that breaks easily.

Holes are formed from gas trapped in the stone as it cools quickly.

Sometimes you will see little bits of volcanic rock or ash caught up in pumice.

The trapped air inside pumice makes the rock very light — it can even float on water!

Pumice rafts

Pumice is often made underwater when volcanoes erupt directly into the sea. Huge rafts of pumice floating on the water often mark the location of these underwater volcanoes!

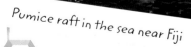

Pumice raft in the sea near Fiji

Diorite

(DIE-or-rite)

Diorite, and the similar rock granodiorite (GRAN-oh-DIE-or-rite), are sometimes described as "salt-and-pepper" igneous rocks thanks to their combinations of light and dark minerals.

Large crystals make these some of the hardest igneous rocks. They are even used to carve granite and other rocks.

Spotty stone

Dalmatian stone is a type of granodiorite from northern Mexico. It has spots of a dark mineral called schorl (SHAWL) on a bed of white feldspar (FELD-spar) – making it look like a spotted Dalmatian dog.

Diorite cools very slowly underground, so it has large crystals.

Anorthosite (an-OR-tho-site) is a rock containing similar minerals to diorite and makes up most of the rock on the Moon!

25

Volcanoes

Volcanoes form where lava sprays out onto the Earth's surface. They are a big part of the Earth's rock cycle, as they are where new igneous rocks are born. Volcanoes come in lots of different shapes and sizes, and can behave in different ways.

Magma that has erupted is known as lava.

This famous volcano in Hawaii is called Mauna Loa. It is made from the igneous rock basalt.

As lava cools, new rocks are formed.

Newly erupted lava is very hot, so it flows down the sides of the volcano.

Lava spattering is a "mini-eruption" of gas released from deep inside the volcano.

If a lava flow hits the ocean it will sometimes shatter into a fine volcanic sand.

Volcanic rocks

Volcanic rocks can show signs of the eruption process. They often contain trapped gas bubbles, bits of glass, or ash. They are also usually fine-grained with no visible crystals because the lava cooled so quickly.

Scoria (SKO-ree-a) is created when tiny bubbles of gas move through lava, which are trapped when the rock cools.

Rhyolite (RYE-oh-lite) forms from a very "sticky" lava, packed with the mineral silica that traps a lot of explosive gas.

Pele's hair (PEL-aze HARE) is made when lava is flung into the air. It "freezes" into strands, much like candy floss, but it is made of glass.

Limestone

(LIME-stone)

Limestone is one of the most important sedimentary rocks. Most types of limestone are made from the shells or skeletons of ancient ocean dwellers, such as shellfish or corals.

Fossils in limestone are the remains of ancient sea animals.

Limestone (LIME-stone)

Living rocks

Many types of limestone are made from the hard parts of sea creatures. Some limestone is made from the hard outer skeletons of coral animals. Chalk is made from the remains of tiny microorganisms with tough shells, called coccoliths.

Coccolith magnified many times

Dolomite (DOLL-oh-mite)

The name dolomite can refer to the rock or the mineral. Dolomite rock is a limestone containing magnesium metal. It is sharp and breaks easily.

Chalk (CHORk)

Chalk is white in colour because it is made mainly from the mineral calcite.

Most limestone types are made up of the minerals aragonite, calcite, and dolomite.

Aragonite (ARA-go-nite)

Calcite (KAL-site)

Dolomite (DOLL-oh-mite)

Travertine (TRAV-er-teen)

Travertine is a banded limestone. It often makes up stalactites and stalagmites.

Travertine terraces

Travertine is a special type of limestone because it isn't made from animal remains. It forms from the mineral calcite dissolved in water. Where there is water with lots of calcite in it, walls of travertine can build up and make beautiful pools.

Travertine pools at Mammoth Hot Springs in Yellowstone National Park, Wyoming, USA

Flint

(FLINT)

Flint is a very sharp rock! It has been used for centuries by humans as an important tool-making material. Flint is hard and easily broken into shards, which allow it to be made into sharp-edged weapons, such as knives, arrowheads, or spear points.

Flint can come in many colours, but it is typically light-coloured tan, brown, or grey.

Like obsidian, flint forms curved surfaces when broken.

Flint is a form of chert, which is a group of rocks made entirely from the mineral quartz.

Chert (CHIRT)

Flint arrowhead

Knap time

Stone Age craftsmen would gather and trade flint from sources far and wide. They carefully chipped it into useful shapes, such as blades. This process is called flint knapping.

Sandstone

(SAND-stone)

Imagine yourself in the time of the dinosaurs, standing on the beach. Those very sands may be preserved as sandstone today! This rock is named after its sand-sized grains — and because many types are made from sand.

Sandstones like these are called picture stones because of the patterns within them.

Bands of red are made of iron oxide, or rust.

Clear layers show where new sediments were added when the rock was made.

Sandstone city

At the historical site of Petra, Jordan, ancient peoples carved an entire city out of large cliffs of rose-pink sandstone. Petra means "rock" in ancient Greek.

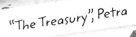

"The Treasury", Petra

Shale

(SHALE)

Shale is the most common sedimentary rock, but sometimes it can be hard to see. Shale is made of soft minerals such as clays, and it breaks up easily. Sometimes, the best way to find shale is to dig down below the soil.

MOST COMMON SEDIMENTARY ROCK

There are no obvious crystals in shale as it is a fine-grained rock.

Shale makes a great place to look for both plant and animal fossils!

Rock power

Shale is a source of oil and gas, such as the oil petroleum (peh-TRO-lee-um), which can be made into fuel. New techniques mean we can access lots more of the petroleum found inside shale rocks than we could before.

Shale contains minerals including clay and quartz.

Clay
(KLAY)

Quartz
(CWOR-ts)

Coal

(COLE)

An important source of energy, coal is burnt in furnaces to help produce electricity. Coal is made of the fossilized remains of plants that lived long ago in swamps or bogs. The deeper and hotter coal is buried, the denser it is, and the more energy it contains.

Plants get their energy from the Sun — so coal can be thought of as "fossilized sunlight"!

There are no obvious crystals in coal.

Coal contains cracks, called cleats, which break up the rock into segments. These cleats form very shiny surfaces.

Anthracite

At high enough depths and temperatures, coal forms anthracite (AN-thra-site). Anthracite coal is very hard and is ¹⁄₁₀th of the thickness of the original pile of plant material it took to make it!

33

Fossils

Fossils are the rocky remains of animals that lived many years ago, and can be great fun to collect. Fossil hunting is every bit as challenging and rewarding as searching for rocks and minerals – and you'll often find them all together.

Trilobites were seafloor dwellers, but they no longer exist. They had segmented shells like lobsters.

Trilobite (TRY-loh-bite)

Types of fossil

The fossils most people think of are dinosaur bones, but all sorts of animals and plant remains can be found. As well as bones and shells, called "body fossils", there is another type of fossil called a "trace fossil". This is evidence of a living thing, such as a dinosaur's footprint.

Brachiopods are shelled animals that have been around for hundreds of millions of years. You can still find them in lakes and oceans.

Brachiopod (BRAY-key-oh-pod)

Crinoid (KRIN-oid)

Crinoids, or "sea lilies", are marine (sea) animals that still exist today! These little wheels are pieces of an ancient crinoid's plant-like stem.

How a fossil forms

Fossilization can occur in many ways. Often, buried bones or shells are replaced by minerals in the water surrounding them. This turns the animal into "stone".

An ammonite meets its end on the ocean floor. It has a hard outer shell, but a soft inside.

Dinosaur claw

Watch out for dinosaur claws! Dinosaur fossils often contain the mineral calcite.

Ammonite (AMMO-nite)

Ammonites were sea creatures related to modern squids. They used their spiralling shell as a floatation device, helping them swim.

Shark's tooth

A shark's tooth like this can be millions of years old and look almost brand new — they can even be sharp!

The insides rot away and the hard shell may be buried by sediments, which may become sedimentary rocks.

New minerals dissolved in the water, such as haematite, may replace minerals in the shell, like calcite or aragonite, making it harder.

Over millions of years, the rock around the fossil wears away (erodes) and allows us to find and collect it!

Marble

(MAHR-bull)

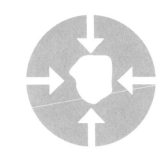

If you have ever seen a historic monument, statue, museum, or palace, chances are you have encountered marble. Marble is formed from limestone, but it is much stronger. It can be cut relatively easily into slabs, making beautiful stones that are sturdy enough to build with.

Quartzite
(CWOR-ts-ite)

Marble
(MAHR-bull)

Quartzite is similar to marble, and the two can sometimes be hard to tell apart! However, quartzite comes from sandstone, not limestone.

Marble often contains "veins" of other types of minerals.

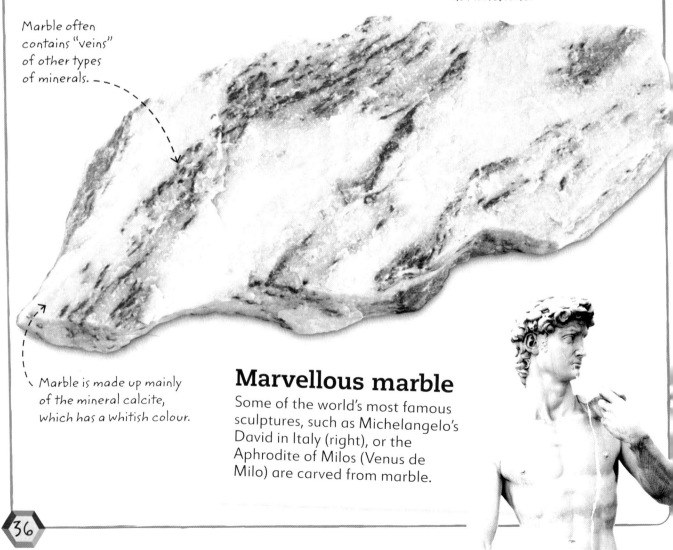

Marble is made up mainly of the mineral calcite, which has a whitish colour.

Marvellous marble

Some of the world's most famous sculptures, such as Michelangelo's David in Italy (right), or the Aphrodite of Milos (Venus de Milo) are carved from marble.

Schist

(SHIST)

If slate is buried deep enough, heat and pressure begin creating new minerals. These new minerals turn the sedimentary slate into metamorphic schist. The minerals form layers stacked one on top of another, known as foliation.

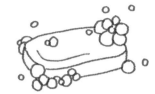

Schists often contain clay minerals such as chlorite (KLOR-rite). Chlorite is very soft, giving the rock a soapy feel.

At high pressures, red garnet (GAR-net) crystals may form in the schist. These rocks look a bit like chocolate chip cookies, with the garnets being the chips!

Some schists sparkle and twinkle! These schists contain the mineral mica (MIKE-a), which is very reflective.

Lapis lazuli

(LAP-iss LAZ-you-lie)

Lapis lazuli is a brilliant blue rock, historically mined in central Asia. Its name literally means "blue stone" in ancient Persian. A lot of the valuable art of ancient civilizations, such as Egypt and Mesopotamia, contained lapis lazuli.

Tutankhamun's eyebrows are made of lapis lazuli!

Tutankhamun

Gold flecks are spots of pyrite.

Lapis lazuli also often contains the mineral sodalite.

The mineral lazurite gives lapis lazuli its blue colour.

Ultrablue

The powdered form of lapis lazuli is called "ultramarine", which was the main source of the deep-blue paint used in oil paintings in the past. It was very expensive, as it was mined in remote areas of Afghanistan!

Gneiss

(NICE)

Gneiss is a rock formed under the highest heat and pressure of all. The layers within it are often squashed into folds or other patterns by the high pressures. The result is a grey, pink, or white rock, with bands resembling a wavy pasta such as lasagna!

Mudstone (MUD-stone)

A mountain to climb

Sedimentary mudstone is often changed into gneiss during mountain building. The heat and pressure first turn these rocks into slate, then schist, then finally into gneiss!

Gneiss contains easy-to-see, thick bands of minerals, which are often folded.

Each layer varies in how thick it is because it has been pushed out of shape.

Slate

(SLAYT)

Slate is a hard, strong rock compared to the shale it is made from. Slate is the first metamorphic rock to be created when sedimentary shale or mudstone experience high heat and pressure.

Useful slate

Slate is a popular building material and has many uses. Pieces of slate were used as the original chalkboards and it is a common material today for floors because it lasts a long time.

Chalkboard

Slate tends to look the same all over, as fossils and other features are destroyed when the rock is heated and squeezed.

Slate is dark-coloured and contains fine lines along its edges.

Hornfels

(HORN-fells)

Hornfels is nature's brick. It is a very hard metamorphic rock that forms when the fine grains of mudstone are "baked" by a nearby source of heat. Unlike other metamorphic rocks, hornfels can be made at lower pressures, closer to the Earth's surface.

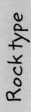

Hornfels is hard and strong, like a brick that has been baked in a kiln (brick oven).

Usually black, brown, or dark green, hornfels often forms cubes or rectangular blocky fragments when broken.

Hornfels can appear banded with stripes.

Hornfels is so tough that in the past it was sometimes used to sharpen knives.

Horn stone

The name "hornfels" is German, and comes from the fact that the rock looks and feels like the horns of an animal, such as a sheep.

Sheep with horns

Uses of rocks

Rocks and minerals are valuable natural resources. Thousands of products that we use every day are made of these materials. For centuries, humans have used rocks for all sorts of things, from making energy to toothpaste.

Rough pumice stones are used to remove dead skin from the feet.

Using a pumice stone

Granite

Pumice

In curling, stones are thrown on ice towards a target.

The stones used in the sport of curling are made from granite from quarries in Scotland and Wales.

Famous landmarks

Tough rocks such as marble have been used for thousands of years in the creation of buildings. Many ancient stone structures are still standing today, and rocks are still used to make all sorts of structures.

El Castillo, a Maya pyramid found at Chichén Itzá, Mexico, is made of limestone and is over 800 years old.

Coal

This marble pestle (stick) and mortar (bowl) is used to grind spices into a powder for use in cooking.

Marble

Coal is an important source of heat energy as it burns easily.

A coal fire

Chalk

Some toothpastes contain chalk, which helps to remove any food on your teeth.

Toothpaste

Over 100 years old, Tower Bridge, which crosses the River Thames in London, UK, is covered in granite and limestone.

The Taj Mahal in Agra, India is a marble tomb built for an emperor's wife. It is over 350 years old.

43

What is a mineral?

A mineral is a solid that contains certain specific chemicals. To be a mineral it must also grow in crystals and be found in nature, but it cannot be made from living things, such as wood.

More than 5,000 minerals have been identified!

What are minerals made of?

Minerals are mixtures of the naturally occurring chemicals, or elements, that make up all known matter in the Universe. Some elements you might already know are the metals iron and copper, as well as the gases oxygen and hydrogen.

The green mineral olivine contains the elements iron, magnesium, silicon, and oxygen.

Olivine (oli-VEEN)

Silicon (sill-i-con)

The second most common element found in minerals is silicon.

Oxygen (OX-ee-gen)

Oxygen is usually found as a gas in the air, but it is also in many minerals.

Types of mineral

Minerals are grouped together based on which chemical elements they contain. For example, the sulphates are a mineral group that contain the element sulphur.

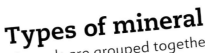

Haematite (HEE-ma-tite)

Haematite is an oxide mineral because it contains the element oxygen and a metal – iron. – – – ➤

Gypsum is an example of a sulphate mineral. It contains sulphur, calcium, and oxygen.

Gypsum (JIP-sum)

Everyday minerals

Minerals are present in our everyday lives. They are in our food, our medicine, the tools we use, and the toys we play with.

Table salt is actually the mineral halite (HA-lite). It forms tiny crystal cubes. – – –

Ice

Salt

Is ice a mineral? Actually, yes it is! It is natural, forms crystals, and is made of the elements oxygen and hydrogen. – – –

Crystals

Mineral crystals are some of the most beautiful things you can find in nature. Crystals have flat faces and straight edges, and many grow in shapes you may recognize. There are six basic types of crystal, shown here.

Pyrite

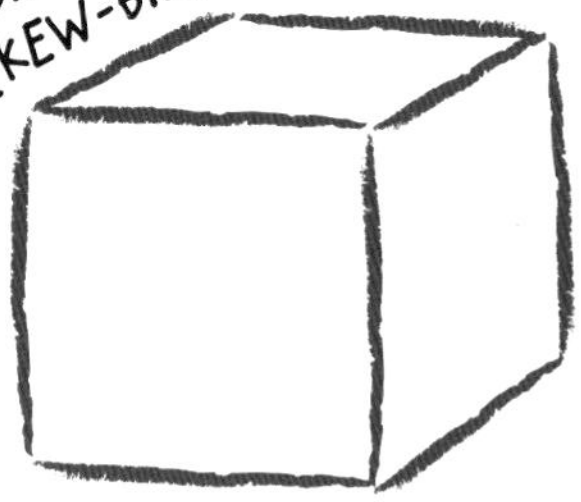

Crystal shapes

Crystals come in a wide variety of shapes. The shape they take is caused by the way the chemicals in them are arranged and the environment in which they grow. This means that natural crystals are rarely perfect.

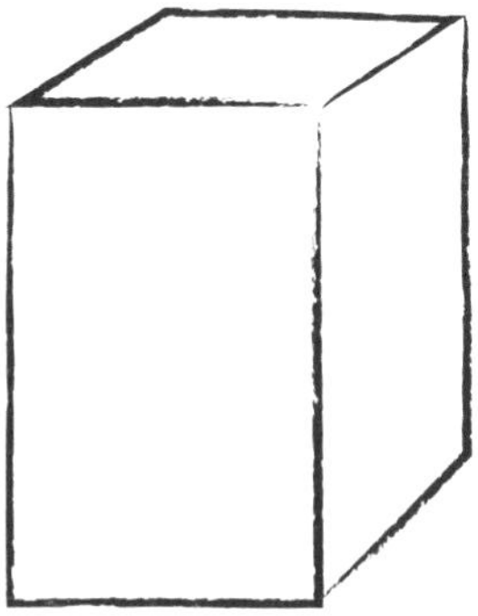

Cubic crystal (KEW-bik)

These pyrite crystals are a classic example of the cubic shape, which has six square faces.

Zircon

Tetragonal crystal (te-TRA-go-nal)

Tetragonal crystals look like a cube that has been "stretched out" to make a cuboid.

Monoclinic crystal (MONO-klin-ik)

Gypsum

Monoclinic crystals have two pairs of opposite sides that are equal lengths. This gypsum crystal looks like a rectangle that has been squashed.

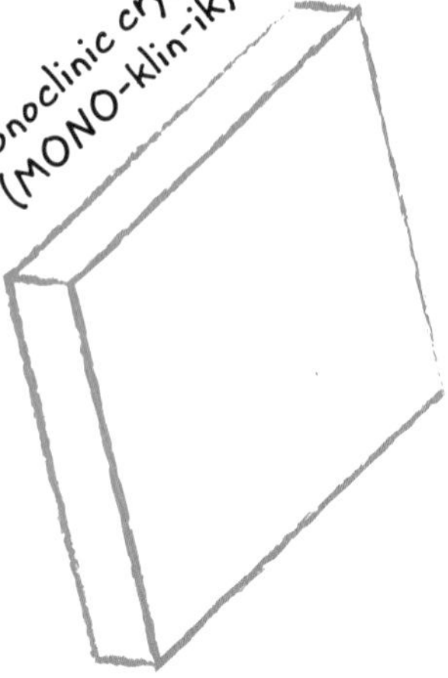

Smoky quartz

Quartz forms hexagonal crystals. They are long with pointed ends, but if you cut them across you would see a hexagon with six sides of equal length.

Axinite

Hexagonal crystal (hex-A-go-nal)

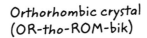

Triclinic crystals can have sides of any length, which means they make unusual shapes.

Triclinic crystal (tri-KLIN-ik)

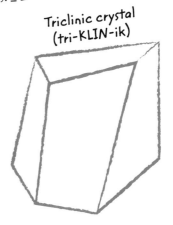

Orthorhombic crystals are similar to tetragonal crystals, but the ends are rectangular, rather than square. Their largest face may point outwards, as on this topaz.

Topaz

Orthorhombic crystal (OR-tho-ROM-bik)

Not a crystal!

If the chemicals in a solid aren't arranged in a particular way, then it will not form crystals. Glass has a more or less random structure so it does not make crystals.

If you look at broken glass, you will see that it typically breaks into randomly shaped pieces. Be careful not to touch it!

Mineral shapes

Rocks and minerals come in all shapes and sizes. Groups of mineral crystals make characteristic shapes, which help us to identify them. We call those shapes their mineral habits.

This mineral contains round, or radial, crystals that look a bit like bicycle wheels!

Fibrous malachite (MAL-a-kite)

Clusters of thin crystals, or fibres, run through this mineral.

Radial wavellite (WAVE-eh-lite)

Tabular muscovite (MUSK-oh-VITE)

Muscovite contains many flat sheets, like the pages of a book. This means it has a tabular habit.

Acicular natrolite (NAY-tro-lite)

Stalactites and stalagmites

Water that has a lot of the mineral calcite in it can drip down from the ceiling of a cave. It then dries into rocky icicles, called stalactites. If the drops are big enough to fall to the floor, they make a stalagmite, which grows up from the ground.

Minerals with delicate, needle-like crystals that look like icicles have an acicular habit.

Stalactites and stalagmites are found in caves made of limestone rocks, which contain the mineral calcite.

Massive turquoise (TURK-oize)

Rosette gypsum (JIP-sum)

Some minerals are plain shapes, appearing as mineral clumps. These are described as having a massive habit.

If crystals form like the petals of a rose, they have a rosette habit.

Identification

Every mineral has its own name, and qualities that help make each one special. However, a mineral won't tell you its name – you'll have to be a rock detective to figure it out!

Cleavage

Cleavage is the ability of certain minerals to break into pieces that have similar shapes to their original shape. If you look closely at crushed salt, you will see it forms tiny cubes, just like the original halite crystal.

Salt

Limonite (LIM-oh-nite) leaves a yellow-brown streak.

A simple porcelain tile makes a great streak plate, but make sure you don't scratch the shiny side of the tile.

Streak test

Even different types of the same mineral will usually have an identical colour when powdered. Rubbing a mineral on an unglazed clay tile and looking at the streak it leaves behind will help you to identify it.

This azurite (AS-you-rite) specimen has a blue streak.

Chrysocolla (KRIS-oh-koh-la) leaves a white or blue-green streak.

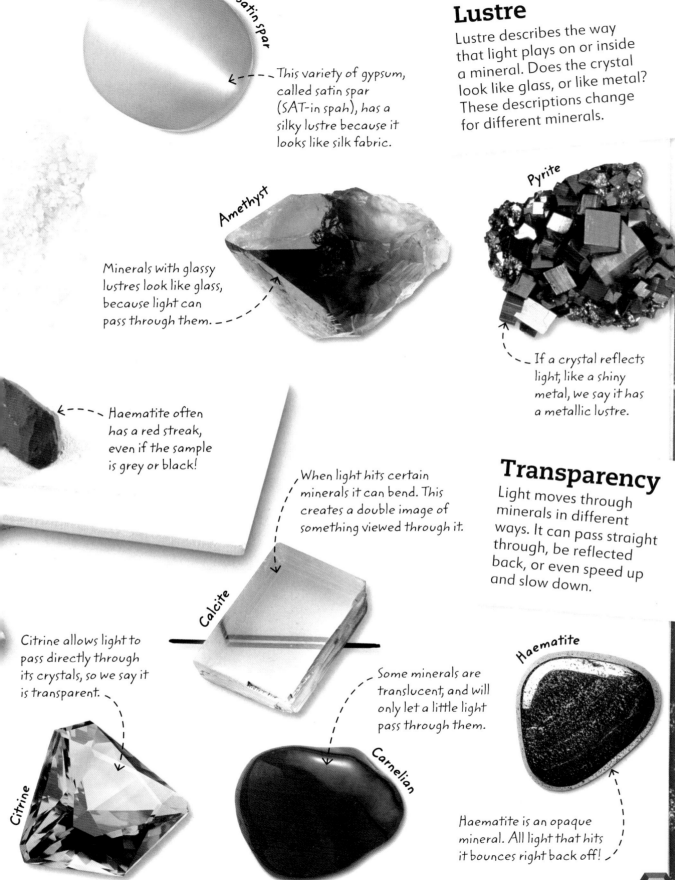

This variety of gypsum, called satin spar (SAT-in spah), has a silky lustre because it looks like silk fabric.

Lustre

Lustre describes the way that light plays on or inside a mineral. Does the crystal look like glass, or like metal? These descriptions change for different minerals.

Satin spar

Amethyst

Minerals with glassy lustres look like glass, because light can pass through them.

Pyrite

If a crystal reflects light, like a shiny metal, we say it has a metallic lustre.

Haematite often has a red streak, even if the sample is grey or black!

When light hits certain minerals it can bend. This creates a double image of something viewed through it.

Transparency

Light moves through minerals in different ways. It can pass straight through, be reflected back, or even speed up and slow down.

Calcite

Citrine allows light to pass directly through its crystals, so we say it is transparent.

Citrine

Some minerals are translucent, and will only let a little light pass through them.

Carnelian

Haematite

Haematite is an opaque mineral. All light that hits it bounces right back off!

51

Calcite (kAL-site)

Each number on the Mohs scale has a particular mineral that has that exact hardness. Calcite has a hardness of 3.

Apatite (A-pa-tite)

Talc (TAL-k)

Gypsum (JIP-sum)

Fluorite (FLOOR-rite)

1

Ice has a hardness of between 1 and 2, so it can scratch talc.

2

A fingernail will scratch gypsum, as it has a hardness of 2.5.

3

A copper coin measures 3.5 on the scale, so it will scratch calcite.

4

At 4.5, a steel nail isn't strong enough to mark apatite.

5

Hard or soft?

The hardness of a mineral helps us to identify it. Hardness is measured using the Mohs scale (shown above), where minerals with higher numbers can scratch minerals with lower numbers.

Diamond can be scratched by two known rare minerals.

Orthoclase (OR-tho-clayze)

Topaz (TOE-pazz)

HARDEST MINERAL!

Diamond (DIE-mond)

Quartz (CWOR-ts)

Corundum (co-RUN-dum)

6

7

8

9

10

Steel files have a hardness of around 6.5, so could scratch all the minerals below them.

Drill bits are designed to be between 7 and 8 on the scale.

Emery boards, used to file nails, often contain corundum mixed with other materials – so they are about 8.5.

Almost nothing can scratch minerals harder than 10!

Glass has a hardness of around 5.5.

Fairy chimneys

In Cappadocia, Turkey, there is a stand of rock stacks known as "fairy chimneys". Hard caps of basalt protected the softer volcanic ash directly below them from being eroded, while the surrounding ash was worn away.

Polishing rocks

Rocks do not always look their best when you find them. However, using the right tools, you can turn the dullest rock into a rock you will want to proudly display. A rock tumbler rolls stones around with grit to make them smooth and shiny.

It takes about 1 month to tumble a gemstone.

Tumbling works best when using stones that don't have too many jagged edges.

Polished stones are smooth and shiny.

Water is added to the tumbler to help break down the rocks.

Water

Dalmatian stone

Jasper

Tiger's eye

Rose quartz

Natural tumbler

Nature's tumblers are streams, rivers, and the sea. The constant action of sand, other stones, and water on rocks wears off any sharp edges and eventually makes a smooth surface.

The buttons are used to set the number of days that the tumbler runs for.

A sieve is used to hold the stones while the grit is washed off.

Sieve

Rocks are constantly on the move in streams.

Electric tumbler

Rock tumblers are used to polish rough stones. They recreate what would happen in a river – moving stones around with water and grit. Larger, sandier grits wear off sharp edges, while finer, powdery grits make the stones shine.

The movement of stones and grit wears away any sharp edges. Each grit (shown below) is tumbled with the stones for around a week.

Inside the barrel

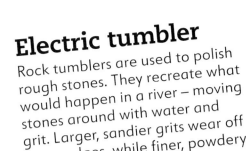

An electric motor turns a belt, which moves the rollers that make the barrel of the tumbler rotate.

Very coarse grit
First, a very coarse, large-grained grit is used to grind off any rough edges.

Coarse grit
Next, a less rough, sand-sized material smoothes the sample down further.

Fine grit
Silt-sized grit is useful for initial polishing. This begins the process of making the rock shiny.

Very fine grit
Finally, a very fine grit, or polish, is used to make the rock really shine!

Quartz

(CWOR-ts)

Quartz is one of the simplest and most common minerals on Earth. It comes in beautiful varieties, many of which have their own names, and are popular with collectors around the world.

Rose quartz gets its rose-red colour from manganese and other metals.

Rose quartz (ROSE CWOR-ts)

Smoky quartz (SMOKE-ee CWOR-ts)

Amethyst grows in pyramid-shaped crystals.

Amethyst is a purple variety of quartz.

Smoky quartz gets its colour from radioactive damage.

Amethyst (A-meh-thist)

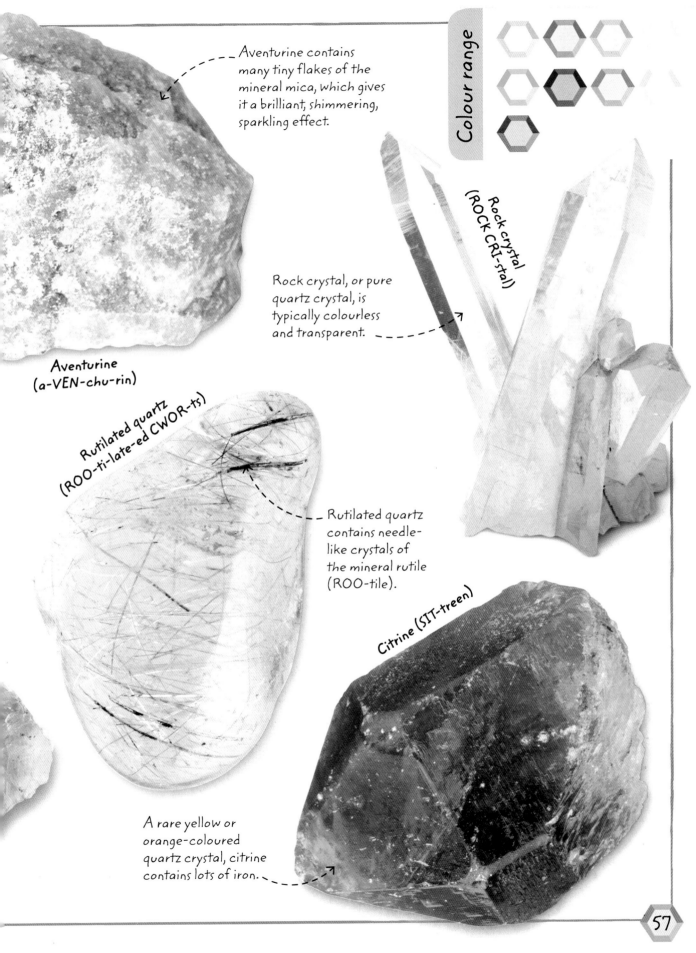

Aventurine contains many tiny flakes of the mineral mica, which gives it a brilliant, shimmering, sparkling effect.

Rock crystal
(ROCK CRI-stal)

Rock crystal, or pure quartz crystal, is typically colourless and transparent.

Aventurine
(a-VEN-chu-rin)

Rutilated quartz
(ROO-ti-late-ed CWOR-ts)

Rutilated quartz contains needle-like crystals of the mineral rutile (ROO-tile).

Citrine (SIT-treen)

A rare yellow or orange-coloured quartz crystal, citrine contains lots of iron.

57

Topaz
(TOE-pazz)

Topaz is a popular mineral and gemstone. It is often yellow, orange, or red, but actually occurs in all colours and can also be colourless. It can be mistaken for quartz, but it is actually much harder than quartz.

Ostro stone from Brazil

Topaz titans

South America is known for its very large topaz crystals. The Ostro stone from Brazil is almost 2 kg (4 lbs). However, some of the largest bits of topaz can weigh hundreds of kilograms!

This topaz has grown in long crystals.

Topaz gets its colour from small amounts of various chemicals.

Topaz is often found alongside fluorite.

Fluorite
(FLOOR-rite)

Amazonite

(AMA-zoh-nite)

Amazonite is a beautiful, but rare, blue-green variety of the mineral microcline (MY-crow-kline). As its name suggests, it was first identified in Brazil near the Amazon River.

The very fine streaks inside the crystal are thin layers of other minerals, which separated from the amazonite when the crystal formed.

Amazonite is found in only a few places, such as Russia, Brazil, and the USA.

The blue-green colour is thought to come from lead metal.

Amazonite, although pretty, is not the best gemstone because its softness means it dulls over time as it scratches easily.

Haematite

(HEE-ma-tite)

Haematite is an iron oxide, which means it is made up of iron and oxygen. Iron oxides can appear very different depending on the amount of iron and oxygen they contain. These minerals are important sources, or ores, of iron.

Paperclips on a piece of magnetite

Magnetic mineral

Iron oxides can have special mineral characteristics, such as magnetism! Magnetite, (MAG-neh-tite), also called lodestone, naturally attracts metal objects such as paperclips.

- - - - Polished haematite is very shiny and reflective.

The planet Mars is red because its surface is covered in iron oxide.

Rust, another iron oxide, forms on the surface of iron objects where it meets oxygen in the air.

Pyrite

(PIE-rite)

Pyrite is also known as "fool's gold" because at first glance it looks similar to gold, but it isn't nearly as valuable. It is a common mineral, but in spite of its name, it is often found alongside real gold.

Pyrite has a metallic lustre.

Its yellow colour makes pyrite look like gold.

This pyrite has a cubic habit with cube-shaped crystals.

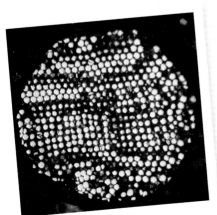

Pyrite framboid

Miniature raspberries

Pyrite is made up of iron and sulphur. If pyrite forms where there is more sulphur than normal, its crystals grow into shapes called framboids. A framboid looks a bit like a tiny raspberry!

Metals from minerals

Shiny metals can be made from some surprisingly dull rocks. Metals are some of the most valuable materials we can get from minerals, as we need them to make all sorts of objects! When a rock or mineral contains metal, it is known as an ore.

The lead in car batteries can come from a mineral ore called galena.

The tin metal used to coat tin cans often comes from an ore called cassiterite.

Tin can

Cassiterite (ka-SITTER-rite)

Galena (gal-EEN-a)

Lead-acid car battery

Panning for gold

Panning for gold

Some metals can be found in pure pieces, not locked away in an ore. These are called "native metals". Small nuggets of native gold can be filtered from mountain streams. Bowls called pans are used to swish the pebbles and water around. Lighter rocks are washed away and the heavier gold is left behind.

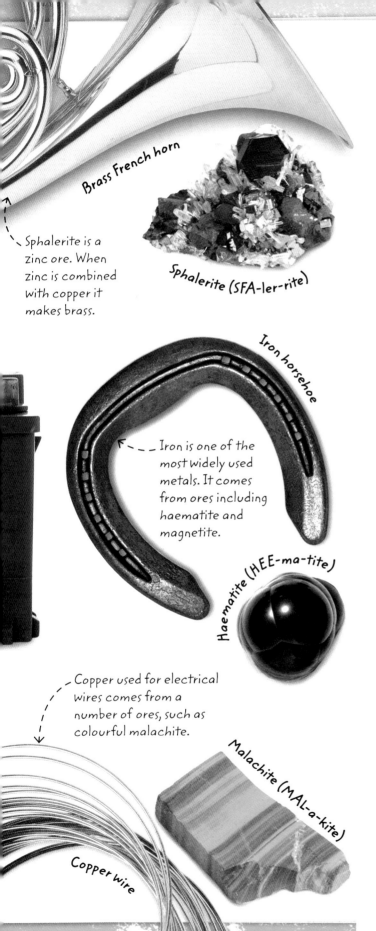

Extracting ores

Metal ores are often dug out of gigantic quarries. Machines on site use heat or special chemicals to remove the metal from the rock. Aluminium is taken from the ore bauxite (BAWK-sight).

Brass French horn

Sphalerite is a zinc ore. When zinc is combined with copper it makes brass.

Sphalerite (SFA-ler-rite)

Iron horsehoe

Iron is one of the most widely used metals. It comes from ores including haematite and magnetite.

Haematite (HEE-ma-tite)

Copper used for electrical wires comes from a number of ores, such as colourful malachite.

Malachite (MAL-a-kite)

Copper wire

The bauxite is first crushed, and then heated and treated with chemicals.

Next, electricity is used to separate liquid aluminium from the other chemicals.

The metal is put into moulds and cooled to create ingots. These can be transported away to make new items.

Kitchen foil is made of aluminium.

Jade

(JAY-d)

The name jade is actually used to refer to one of two minerals – jadeite (JAY-dite) or nephrite (NEF-rite). These have both been used for thousands of years. Carving jade was common for the Aztec and Maya peoples, as well as in the cultures of Japan, China, Mongolia, and Korea.

Nephrite

Nephrite is slightly softer than jadeite, so it is sometimes called "soft jade".

This jadeite is a pale, pearly green colour.

Green gold

In ancient China, jade was more valuable than gold or diamonds. It was used as a sign of royalty or wealth. Jade's strong but carveable hardness mean many beautiful pieces of Chinese jade have survived – this piece is thought to be over 300 years old.

Jadeite has a glassy or greasy lustre.

Tourmaline

(TORE-ma-leen)

Tourmaline is a semi-precious gemstone often found near granite. It is actually a family of minerals with more than 32 varieties, many of which come in different colours. It is a very brittle mineral, which means it breaks easily.

Colour range

Watermelon

Tourmaline that is pink and green is called "watermelon tourmaline".

Pink tourmaline is called rubellite (ROO-beh-lite).

Tourmaline often forms three-sided crystals.

Green tourmaline is called verdelite (VER-deh-lite).

Pegmatites

Tourmalines are often found in pegmatites. Pegmatites are cracks in the Earth's surface in which magma has formed minerals with large crystals. These pegmatites can be found around the world, often with granite.

Mica

(MIKE-a)

Micas are a group of very common minerals. They are made of layers of many flat, sheet-like crystals that make "books". Mica "books" can be beautiful additions to any collection – if you can resist the urge to peel them apart!

You can peel the layers down to the level of one atom thick, in theory, but you will need a really sharp fingernail!

This pale mica is called muscovite (MUSK-oh-VITE).

The crystals in this muscovite mica form flat, hexagonal (six-sided) shapes.

Each crystal forms a "book" that can be peeled into individual sheets.

Mica windows

Thin muscovite micas are transparent to translucent, which means light can pass through them. In the past, sheets of muscovite were sometimes used in place of glass for windows or mirrors.

Moonstone

(MOON-stone)

Moonstone got its name because it reflects light to produce the effect of "moonlight dancing on water". If you turn a moonstone as you look inside it you will see the same patterns of light that amazed the Ancient Romans and Greeks, who once worshipped the stone!

The Ancient Romans thought that moonstone was moonlight made into stone.

The effect of light on a moonstone actually has a name — it is called the schiller.

Moonstones can be cut and polished to help them reflect the light.

Ultrafine layers of a mineral called adularia (A-due-LAIR-ria), are what reflect the light.

Polished moonstone

Chalcedony

(kal-SED-oh-nee)

Chalcedony is a form of quartz with very tiny crystals. Each crystal is impossible to see without special equipment. Unlike varieties of quartz with large crystals, such as amethyst, chalcedony varieties are usually smooth and glassy.

Also known as "sard", carnelian is translucent, which means you can see light coming through it. Its blood-red colour comes from small amounts of iron.

Carnelian (car-NEE-lee-an)

Also called "heliotrope", bloodstone is a type of green jasper with flecks of red haematite floating in it.

Jasper (JA-spur)

Bloodstone (BLUD-stone)

Jasper is opaque, so you can't see through its crystals. It is often brown, yellow, or red due to traces of iron.

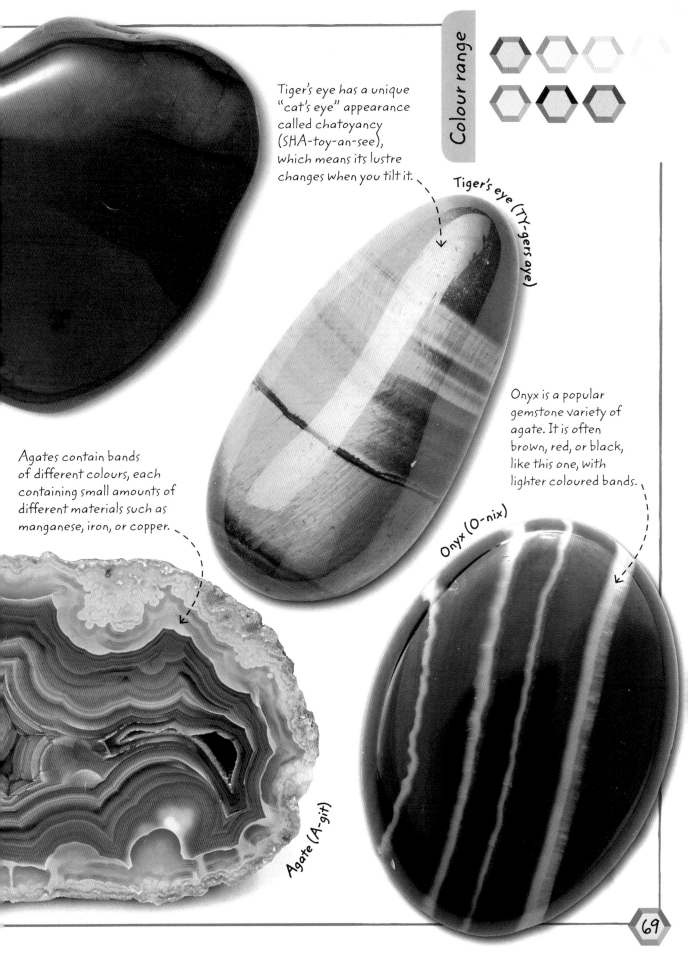

Tiger's eye has a unique "cat's eye" appearance called chatoyancy (SHA-toy-an-see), which means its lustre changes when you tilt it.

Tiger's eye (TY-gers aye)

Onyx is a popular gemstone variety of agate. It is often brown, red, or black, like this one, with lighter coloured bands.

Agates contain bands of different colours, each containing small amounts of different materials such as manganese, iron, or copper.

Onyx (O-nix)

Agate (A-git)

69

Geodes

A geode is a rock with an empty space inside it that is lined with crystals. Geodes are a type of vug, which are the cavities inside rocks that sometimes have a mineral coating. Vugs can be small, like geodes, or large underground caves such as the Cave of Crystals in Mexico.

This cave is made of limestone. It is found along a deep crack in the mountain above.

The crystals formed when a hot liquid containing dissolved minerals slowly cooled inside the cave. Scientists pumped the liquid out so the space could be explored.

A nearby magma chamber provided the heat to make the mineral-filled liquid that made the crystals.

The selenite crystals in the cave can be 11 m (36 ft) long and 1 m (3 ft) wide.

Scientists must wear protective gear due to the extreme heat and humidity in the cave.

How a geode forms

Sometimes, water containing dissolved minerals seeps into hollow spaces in a rock. The minerals form crystals as the water releases them, slowly coating the inner surface of the rock. Geodes are usually found inside basalt or limestone.

Unbroken geodes don't often look like much. As the rock around it wears away, a roughly round, potato-like stone is left.

Once cut or broken you can see the crystals lining the inside. This amethyst geode is filled with minerals grown from water passing through it.

Garnet

(GAR-net)

There are six minerals that make up the garnet family and many are red. Pieces of garnet were some of the earliest gemstones to be traded, not just for their beauty, but because some are hard enough to grind down softer gems.

There are 5 more main types of garnet:

Pyrope
(PIE-rope)

Almandine
(AL-man-deen)

Spessartite
(SPESS-a-tite)

Andradite
(AN-dra-dite)

Uvarovite
(OO-va-roe-vite)

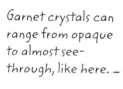

Garnet crystals can range from opaque to almost see-through, like here.

This type of garnet is called grossular (GROS-you-lar).

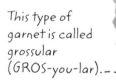

Garnets are most commonly found in 12-sided spheres, and look like red footballs!

When grossular is a reddish brown colour it is known as "cinnamon stone".

Labradorite

(lab-RA-door-ite)

Labradorite is famous to collectors for its unique iridescence in light. Iridescence is the separation of white light into different colours by the mineral's crystals – just as raindrops split light to make a rainbow.

Iridescence in labradorite is called "labradorescence".

The reflection of light is similar to the iridescence in moonstone.

Polishing the mineral's surface will allow light to enter the rock and help to produce the best iridescent effect.

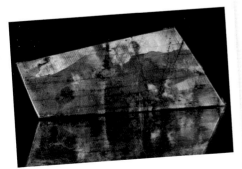

Spectrolite

Rainbow rock

One rare variety of labradorite, called spectrolite (SPEK-troh-lite), has a high level of labradorescence and a large range of colours – including reds, oranges, yellows, and violets.

73

Sodalite

(SODE-a-lite)

Sodalite is a deep-blue coloured mineral that contains the metal sodium. Like halite (rock salt), which is also made of sodium, sodalite is light and breaks easily, so it often contains many cracks. It is one of the minerals found inside the rock lapis lazuli.

Lazurite (LAZ-you-rite)

Sodalite is similar to the mineral lazurite that gives lapis lazuli its colour, but it is less valuable.

The white patches are not part of the sodalite mineral, but are from the rock it formed in.

Sodalite has a royal-blue colour.

Soft rock

Don't carry sodalite in your pocket, or store it with other minerals, as it will scratch easily. However, even though it is soft it can be cut into gemstones.

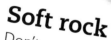

Sodalite may smell bad if you break it, as it often contains sulphur —the same chemical as in rotten eggs!

Turquoise

(TURK-oize)

Turquoise is a popular gemstone found in Turkey, which lends its name to the mineral's characteristic colour. It is also found in the Middle East, Mexico, and the USA. Along with lapis lazuli and jade, turquoise is one of the oldest-known gems to be traded long distances.

Turquoise Aztec mask

Ancient wonder

Turquoise has been popular for thousands of years with the Mayas, Aztecs, Persians, and Mesopotamians.

Turquoise crystals have no defined shape. They are not able to be seen without a microscope, and even then they may be difficult to find.

Turquoise has a soft bluish or greenish colour.

Turquoise is commonly used to make jewellery and sculptures.

This turquoise stone has veins of iron oxide running through it.

Fluorite

(FLOOR-rite)

Fluorite, also called "fluorospar", can be colourless or a variety of rare colours. It is found around the world, often in the same place as other valuable crystals that a rockhound might be in search of. It shows you when you are hunting in a good place, which makes it a great "indicator" mineral.

Fluorite glows under ultraviolet light.

Fluorite comes in many colours, even in the same crystal, like the thin purple lines here.

This mineral grows in cubic crystals.

Fluorite is sometimes known for its blue to purple colour.

Blue John

Blue John is a particularly famous variety of purple and blue fluorite. It has been mined since the 18th century near Derbyshire, England. It is very popular for ornamental stones and is still mined today.

Blue John cup

76

Rhodonite

(ROD-oh-nite)

Rhodonite is a gemstone with pink or rose-red crystals that can rival the deep colour of rubies. In fact, "rhodon" means rose in Ancient Greek. Rhodonite is an ore of the metal manganese, which gives it its pink colour.

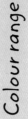

Imposter

Rhodochrosite (ROH-doh-CROW-site) is similar – and often mistaken for – rhodonite. However, gem cutters often prefer to work with rhodonite rather than rhodochrosite because it is harder and doesn't wear down as fast.

There are no obvious crystals in this piece of rhodonite.

Rhodonite has a glassy lustre.

The manganese in rhodonite turns black when exposed to the air.

Glow in the dark

Some rock collections have a surprising secret – certain minerals can glow under special "black lights" that give off ultraviolet (UV) light. The ability of some minerals to glow in the dark is called fluorescence.

Fluorescence is named after the mineral fluorite.

UV light reacts with ingredients in minerals called "activators" to make them shine. Fluorine is an activator that makes fluorite glow blue.

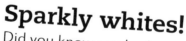

Fluorite

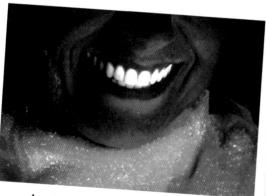

Apatite in teeth glowing in UV light

Sparkly whites!

Did you know you had minerals in your head? Apatite is a mineral found in your teeth! It contains the activator fluorine, which causes them to glow bright white in UV light.

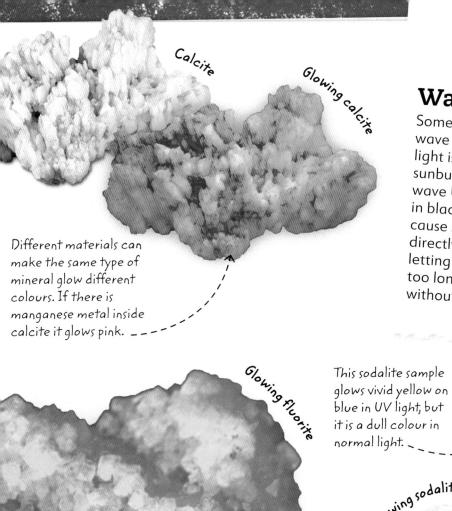

Calcite

Glowing calcite

Different materials can make the same type of mineral glow different colours. If there is manganese metal inside calcite it glows pink.

Black light

Warning!

Some rock shops also sell short-wave UV lights. Short-wave UV light is the same light that causes sunburn on a sunny day. Long-wave UV light, like the kind found in black lights, typically will not cause sunburn. Avoid looking directly at short-wave UV lights, or letting them shine on your skin for too long. Never use a UV light without an adult to help you.

Glowing fluorite

This sodalite sample glows vivid yellow on blue in UV light, but it is a dull colour in normal light.

Sodalite

Glowing sodalite

Glowing adamite

Adamite

Adamite (AD-a-mite) glows green in UV light.

Cutting gems

Gemstones are naturally dazzling, but if they are shaped or cut, light can bounce around inside them, giving them even more sparkle. Gems are cut by gem cutters called lapidaries.

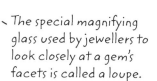

Jeweller's loupe

The special magnifying glass used by jewellers to look closely at a gem's facets is called a loupe.

Raw stone

The raw gemstone being polished and cut here is cubic zirconia (KEW-bik zer-CO-nee-a). Raw gems are chosen for their clarity, which means they don't have any cracks or chips in them.

Raw cubic zirconia

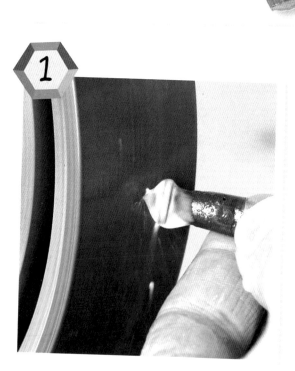

The first step is to grind the raw stone into the rough shape it will be, using a grinding wheel. The gem is held in place on a holder called a dop stick, which is coated in wax.

Next, it is important to make sure the top of the stone, which is known as the table, is perfectly flat. To do this it is checked by eye against a grid.

Water dripped onto the wheel prevents dust from escaping.

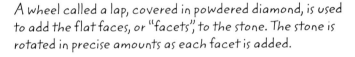

4

A wheel called a lap, covered in powdered diamond, is used to add the flat faces, or "facets", to the stone. The stone is rotated in precise amounts as each facet is added.

The facets are then polished using a lap with an even finer diamond powder. The polished facets look much shinier.

5

Finished stone

Sparkling gem

After some hard work and patience, the cut gem is ready to be used in jewellery. This type of cut is called a brilliant cut, as it makes the gem sparkle.

Once the top surface is finished, the point of the gem, called the pavilion, can be faceted and polished as well.

The gem is attached to the dop stick with sticky wax.

Precious gems

The most prized gemstones are ones that are hard to find, have no flaws, and are big! When carefully prepared by polishing and cutting, gems can become brilliant and valuable jewels. Jewels are a common sign of wealth or status in many cultures.

Rays of light enter the gem.

The light bounces off the surfaces inside the gem.

Cut brilliantly

Jewels are cut to make sure they reflect all the light that enters them. This is what makes them twinkle and sparkle. This diagram shows how light might bounce inside a "brilliant cut" gem, which is a gem with many facets and a pointed base.

Sapphire

Some sapphires can change colour depending on the angle that you look at them.

Diamonds are one of the most valuable gems. They are not as rare as you think, but few are flawless, with no cracks or marks inside them.

Diamond

Ruby

Gems can be classified as either "precious", like this ruby, or "semi-precious", like agate.

Opal

Most opals, like this one, are green and blue. However, the most valuable are black opals from Australia.

Synthetic gemstones

Not all gemstones are found in nature. Modern techniques allow artificial minerals to be "grown" in laboratories. These are known as "synthetic" (sin-thet-ik) gems.

It can be very hard to tell the difference between a natural and synthetic gem.

Synthetic ruby

Synthetic emerald

Synthetic opal

Emeralds are a green type of the mineral beryl. They are often paired with diamonds to create expensive jewellery.

Emerald

Priceless gems

Some gems, like the Pink Star diamond, are extremely rare and beautiful. Gems are weighed in "carats", with each carat being 0.2 g (0.007 oz). The Pink Star diamond is almost 60 carats, and a rare pink colour. Auction bids for it in 2013 reached over $83 million.

The Pink Star diamond

Living gems

Gems aren't alive, but they might once have been! Some gemstones are distant relatives of ancient trees and animals. Remains of these life forms can even end up stuck inside rocks.

Carved jet

Like coal, jet is made of wood that has been squashed over many years. Its shiny surface is prized for carvings.

Raw jet

Amber

Growing a gem

Living things make many materials that people can use as gemstones or in jewellery. Sea creatures make pearls, while over many years, trees can become beautiful gemstones themselves.

Very similar to amber, copal is also made from tree resin. However, it is not as old as amber and is only partly fossilized.

Trees make resin to seal wounds in their bark.

Copal

Amber is made out of fossilized tree resin. It often contains insects that were trapped in the sticky, liquid resin millions of years ago.

Over many years, the living parts of this tree have been replaced with minerals such as calcite or silica, turning it to stone – or "petrifying" it. You can still see the rings inside the trunk.

Petrified wood

Oysters and mussels make a natural substance called nacre (NAY-ker), which forms shiny shells and beautiful pearls.

Pearls

Oyster

The nacre that forms pearls contains the mineral aragonite and has a shiny lustre.

Paua shell

Some sea snails also produce nacre. This paua shell has been polished to reveal the colourful nacre underneath.

How a pearl is made

A pearl is a true treasure of the sea! Pearls are created by shelled creatures, such as oysters, that live underwater. Pearls are often used to make earrings and necklaces because of their beautiful lustre.

Some bivalves have a shiny coating inside their shells called "mother of pearl", or "nacre" (NAY-ker).

A hard shell protects the oyster's soft body.

What is an oyster?

An oyster is a type of mollusc called a bivalve. Bivalves are related to garden slugs and snails, but they live underwater and have a hinged shell. Oysters live on the ocean floor, filtering tiny creatures from the water to eat.

How a pearl forms

If a bit of grit gets inside an oyster's shell, it will make a pearl around it in order to contain it. Pearls are made of the nacre an oyster makes to coat the inside of its shell. Round pearls are valuable because they are relatively rare.

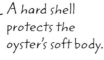

Pearls are made inside the oyster's shell.

Sometimes a piece of grit will work its way inside an oyster and get stuck.

1

Farming pearls

Many pearls you see in shops are cultured pearls that have been grown at an oyster farm. On a farm, material is deliberately put inside the oyster's shell so it makes a pearl.

Pearl oysters being farmed

Pearl necklace

Some pearls contain other materials, giving them unusual colours.

If a pearl gets stuck to the shell it is called a blister pearl.

Freshwater

Pearls made by oysters are called saltwater pearls, but some mussels that live in lakes and streams can make pearls too — called freshwater pearls.

2 In response, the oyster creates a "pearl sac" around it, which coats the grit in layers of nacre.

3 Over years, and repeated coatings, the grain builds up into a solid smooth ball — a pearl.

Birthstones

The tradition of matching certain stones to one of the 12 calendar months has existed for thousands of years, but the specific stones have changed over time. Your "birthstone" is the stone of the month you were born in.

Turquoise
Turquoise is the birthstone for December, but zircon or tanzanite are also used.

Topaz
Topaz and citrine are November's birthstones.

December

November

Opal
Opal is October's birthstone, as is tourmaline.

October

Gems, such as these pearls, make valuable necklaces or bracelets.

Sapphire
Sapphire is a blue type of the mineral corundum.

September

August

July

Peridot
Peridot is the gem for August. It is a type of the mineral olivine.

Gem-quality minerals such as opal make brilliant stones for setting in rings.

Ruby
Rubies are red crystals of the mineral corundum.

Garnet
The garnet group has many varieties, most of which are red.

January

Amethyst
This colourful variety of quartz is February's birthstone.

February

The Black Star of Queensland is a huge black sapphire.

March

Aquamarine
Aquamarine is a blue variety of the mineral beryl.

April

Diamond
The birthstone for April is diamond. In the UK, rock crystal (quartz) is also used.

May

Amethysts can be set into earrings. - - ↘

June

Pearl
Pearls, or sometimes moonstone, are used to represent June.

Emerald
May's birthstone is emerald — a deep-green variety of the mineral beryl.

All together

This book barely scratches the surface of the thousands of rocks and minerals in the world. Here you'll find a selection of the specimens shown in the book, and how to say them.

Agate
(A-git)
pg. 69

Almandine
(AL-man-deen)
pg. 72

Amazonite
(AMA-zoh-nite)
pg. 59

Amethyst
(A-meh-thist)
pg. 56

Andradite
(AN-dra-dite)
pg. 72

Anthracite
(AN-thra-site)
pg. 33

Aragonite
(ARA-go-nite)
pg. 29

Aventurine
(a-VEN-chu-rin)
pg. 57

Basalt
(BA-salt)
pg. 22

Bloodstone
(BLUD-stone)
pg. 68

Calcite
(KAL-site)
pg. 29

Carnelian
(car-NEE-lee-an)
pg. 68

Chalk
(CHORK)
pg. 29

Chert
(CHIRT)
pg. 30

Citrine
(SIT-treen)
pg. 57

Clay
(KLAY)
pg. 32

Coal
(COLE)
pg. 33

Dalmatian stone
(DAL-may-shun stone)
pg. 25

Diorite
(DIE-or-rite)
pg. 25

Dolomite
(DOLL-oh-mite)
pg. 28

Dolomite
(DOLL-oh-mite)
pg. 29

Epidote
(EP-ee-doh-t)
pg. 23

Feldspar
(FELD-spar)
pg. 20

Flint
(FLINT)
pg. 30

Fluorite
(FLOOR-rite)
pg. 76

Gabbro
(GAB-roe)
pg. 22

Garnet
(GAR-net)
pg. 72

Gneiss
(NICE)
pg. 39

Granite
(GRAN-it)
pg. 20

Grossular
(GROS-you-lar)
pg. 72

Haematite
(HEE-ma-tite)
pg. 60

Hornfels
(HORN-fells)
pg. 41

Jadeite
(JAY-dite)
pg. 64

Jasper
(JA-spur)
pg. 68

Labradorite
(lab-RA-door-ite)
pg. 73

Lapis lazuli
(LAP-iss
LAZ-you-lie)
pg. 38

Lazurite
(LAZ-you-rite)
pg. 74

Limestone
(LIME-stone)
pg. 28

Marble
(MAHR-bull)
pg. 36

Mica
(MIKE-a)
pg. 66

Moonstone
(MOON-stone)
pg. 67

Mudstone
(MUD-stone)
pg. 39

Nephrite
(NEF-rite)
pg. 64

Obsidian
(ob-SID-ee-an)
pg. 21

Onyx
(O-nix)
pg. 69

Pegmatite
(PEG-ma-tite)
pg. 65

Pumice
(PUM-iss)
pg. 24

Pyrite
(PIE-rite)
pg. 61

Pyrope
(PIE-rope)
pg. 72

Quartz
(CWOR-ts)
pg. 56

Quartzite
(CWOR-ts-ite)
pg. 36

Rhodochrosite
(ROH-doh-
CROW-site)
pg. 77

Rhodonite
(ROD-oh-nite)
pg. 77

**Rock
crystal**
(ROCK CRI-stal)
pg. 57

**Rose
quartz**
(ROSE
CWOR-ts)
pg. 56

**Rutilated
quartz**
(ROO-ti-late-ed
CWOR-ts)
pg. 57

Sandstone
(SAND-stone)
pg. 31

Schist
(SHIST)
pg. 37

Shale
(SHALE)
pg. 32

Slate
(SLAYT)
pg. 40

**Smoky
quartz**
(SMOKE-ee
CWOR-ts)
pg. 56

**Snowflake
obsidian**
(SNOW-flake
ob-SID-ee-an)
pg. 21

Sodalite
(SODE-a-lite)
pg. 74

Spectrolite
(SPEK-troh-lite)
pg. 73

Spessartite
(SPESS-a-tite)
pg. 72

Tiger's eye
(TY-gers aye)
pg. 69

Topaz
(TOE-pazz)
pg. 58

Tourmaline
(TORE-ma-leen)
pg. 65

Travertine
(TRAV-er-teen)
pg. 29

Turquoise
(TURK-oize)
pg. 75

Unakite
(OON-a-KITE)
pg. 23

Uvarovite
(OO-va-roe-vite)
pg. 72

Glossary

chatoyancy
Effect when certain minerals are tilted and they reflect a strip of light that looks like the shine of a cat's eye.

cleavage
Ability of a mineral to break into smaller pieces that have the same shape of the original mineral.

conchoidal fracturing
Tendency for some minerals to break into smooth, curved shapes, like a conch shell.

core
Innermost section of the Earth, made up of a solid, inner layer of iron and nickel, and a liquid outer layer.

crust
Cold, hard, outer layer of the Earth, where all known life exists.

crystal
Piece of a mineral with a recognizable shape, such as a cube.

element
One of 118 known substances that make up all known materials, including minerals.

erosion
Break up and movement of pieces of rock called sediments by water, wind, or weather.

facet
Cut face of a gemstone.

fluorescence
Ability of a mineral to give off light that can be seen when exposed to rays of invisible ultraviolet light.

fossil
Preserved remains, or evidence of, ancient life, found in many sedimentary rocks.

gemstone
Rock or mineral that has value when cut and polished, including precious (highly valuable) and semi-precious (less valuable) stones.

geode
Open cavity or vug that is found within a single rock, which may be filled later with mineral crystals.

grit
Fine grains of rough material, used in the grinding and polishing of rocks and minerals in a tumbler.

habit
Typical shape in which a certain mineral will grow. Examples are tabular – tablet or book-like shapes, and acicular – needle-like shapes.

igneous
Type of rock that is formed by the cooling of magma or lava, either deep inside the Earth or at a volcano.

lapidary
Art of cutting, polishing, or carving rough stones into gems, jewellery, and other decorative items.

lava
Magma that has erupted at the Earth's surface.

lustre
Description of how light reflects off a mineral's surface.

magma
Molten rock created in the upper mantle, deep below the surface of the Earth.

mantle

Middle and thickest layer of the Earth. The inner mantle is made of liquid rock. The outer mantle is made of rock that is more like toothpaste.

metamorphic

Type of rock formed when heat and pressure change the structure of rock that already exists.

mineral

Naturally occurring solid made of crystals. Minerals are made up of specific combinations of elements.

Mohs scale

Scale showing the relative hardness of one mineral to another. Talc is the softest mineral with a value of 1, and diamond is the hardest with a value of 10.

nacre

Also called "mother of pearl", a coating produced by shellfish, which forms the shiny coating of a pearl.

native

Naturally occurring metal.

ore

Rock or mineral from which a metal can be obtained.

petrify

Process of replacing a living material, such as wood, with minerals. It literally means "to turn into stone".

rock

Solid mixture of minerals and other solids. Rocks form in three types: igneous, sedimentary, and metamorphic.

rock cycle

Process by which the Earth transforms igneous, sedimentary, and metamorphic rocks into other types of rock.

rock tumbler

Machine used to smooth and polish rough-cut minerals and rocks into semi-precious gemstones.

rockhound

Person who loves to hunt, collect, and admire rocks, gems, minerals, and fossils.

rough

Uncut, unpolished rock for use in rock tumbling and lapidary.

sedimentary

Type of rock formed by the weathering and erosion of existing rock to sediments, which are deposited in an ocean or lake to form a new rock layer.

schiller

Effect in which the inside of a gem appears to flash with light when turned.

streak

Coloured powder left behind when mineral specimens are rubbed on a porcelain plate.

weathering

When wind, water, and air physically break down a rock into smaller pieces, or sediments, or when rocks chemically dissolve in water.

vug

Any open hole or cavity in a rock or rock formation, such as a geode or cave.

Index

Acknowledgements

Dorling Kindersley would like to thank Megan Weal for editorial assistance, Bettina Myklebust Stovne for illustration, Polly Goodman for proofreading, and Helen Peters for the index. The publishers would also like to thank Richard Leeney for photography, Holts Gems and Roger Dunkin for allowing us to photograph gem cutting, and Sam Moore for lending us his fantastic rock collection for us to photograph. The author would like to thank his wife, Elizabeth Dennie, for her valuable editorial assistance on this book.

The publisher would like to thank the following for their kind permission to reproduce their photographs:

(Key: a-above; b-below/bottom; c-centre; f-far; l-left; r-right; t-top)

2 Dorling Kindersley: Holts Gems (bc). **3 Dorling Kindersley**: Natural History Museum, London (tc). **4 Dorling Kindersley**: Natural History Museum, London (br). **5 Dorling Kindersley**: Natural History Museum, London (br). **6 Alamy Stock Photo**: B.A.E. Inc. (cr). **7 Dorling Kindersley**: Natural History Museum, London (cl). **8-9 Alamy Stock Photo**: Federico Rostagno. **9 Dorling Kindersley**: Natural History Museum, London (br). **iStockphoto.com**: Mypurgatoryyears (bl). **10 Dorling Kindersley**: Natural History Museum, London (cl, clb). **12 Dorling Kindersley**: RHS and garden designer. (cr). **13 Dorling Kindersley**: Natural History Museum, London (bc). 16 Alamy Stock Photo: John Cancalosi (bl). **17 Dorling Kindersley**: Trustees of the National Museums Of Scotland (bl). **18 iStockphoto.com**: SumikoPhoto (cr). **19 Alamy Stock Photo**: Kevin Ebi (c). **20 Dorling Kindersley**: Natural History Museum, London (c, crb). **22 Dorling Kindersley**: National Trust (bl). 23 **iStockphoto.com**: VvoeVale (cra). **24 Alamy Stock Photo**: David Fleetham (bl). **26-27 Alamy Stock Photo**: Phil Degginger. **27 Dorling Kindersley**: Natural History Museum, London (crb); The Science Museum, London (cra). **28 Alamy Stock Photo**: Natural History Museum, London (clb). Dorling Kindersley: Natural History Museum, London (cra). **29 Dorling Kindersley**: Natural History Museum, London (cl). iStockphoto.com: julof90 (br). 31 Alamy Stock Photo: Leon Werdinger (c). **33 Dorling Kindersley**: Trustees of the National Museums Of Scotland and Trustees of the National Museums Of Scotland and Trustees of the National Museums Of Scotland (c). **35 Dorling Kindersley**: Natural History Museum, London (tc, crb). **36 Alamy Stock Photo**: RF Company (c). **Dorling Kindersley**: Natural History Museum, London (cra). **Getty Images**: Alxpin (br). **38 Dorling Kindersley**: Cairo Museum (cra). **41 Alamy Stock Photo**: Siim Sepp (c). **42 123RF.com**: 36clicks (clb). iStockphoto.com: MileA (c). **43 Alamy Stock Photo**: Joanne Millington (cla); WidStock (tl). **44 iStockphoto.com**: Kerrick (clb). **45 Alamy Stock Photo**: D. Hurst (bc). **46 Dorling Kindersley**: Natural History Museum, London (c). **47 Dorling Kindersley**: Natural History Museum, London (tl, tr, bl). **49 Alamy Stock Photo**: Falk Kienas (cra); RF Company (tl). **51 Dorling Kindersley**: Holts Gems (bl); Natural History Museum, London (cra, tl). **52 Dorling Kindersley**: Natural History Museum, London (tc, tr). 53 123RF.com: Derege (br). **Dorling Kindersley**: Natural History Museum, London (tl, cla, tc, tr, cra). **56 Dorling Kindersley**: Natural History Museum, London (bl). **58 Alamy Stock Photo**: Roger Bacon (cra); Phil Degginger / Jack Clark Collection (cb). **Dorling Kindersley**: Natural History Museum, London (br). **59 Dorling Kindersley**: Natural History Museum, London (c). **60 iStockphoto.com**: Mailmyworkdd (br). **Science Photo Library**: Albert Copley, Visuals Unlimited (cra). **61 Alamy Stock Photo**: Linda Reinink-Smith (bl). **62 Dorling Kindersley**: Natural History Museum, London (clb, cr). **62-63 Dorling Kindersley**: Exide Batteries Ltd (c). **63 Alamy Stock Photo**: Panda Eye (crb); Friedrich Stark (cra); Simon Turner (cr). **64 Alamy Stock Photo**: Museum of East Asian Art (bl). **Dorling Kindersley**: Holts Gems (c). **65 Dorling Kindersley**: Natural History Museum, London (c). **66 Alamy Stock Photo**: Valery Voennyy (br). **67 Dorling Kindersley**: Holts Gems (br); Natural History Museum, London (c). **68 Dorling Kindersley**: Holts Gems (c). **68-69 Alamy Stock Photo**: Natural History Museum, London (bc). **70-71 Getty Images**: Carsten Peter / Speleoresearch & Films (cra). **71 123RF.com**: Fotointeractiva (cra). **Alamy Stock Photo**: Ingo Schulz (crb). **72 123RF.com**: Dipressionist (bl). **Dorling Kindersley**: Holts Gems (cr); Natural History Museum, London (crb, br). **73 Alamy Stock Photo**: Henri Koskinen (bl). **74 Dorling Kindersley**: Natural History Museum, London (bl). **75 Alamy Stock Photo**: World History Archive (cra). **76 Dorling Kindersley**: Oxford University Museum of Natural History (br). **78 Science Photo Library**: Cordelia Molloy (bl). **79 Dorling Kindersley**: The Science Museum, London (crb, cr). **80 Dorling Kindersley**: Holts Gems (tc, ca, tr, c, clb, crb); Natural History Museum, London (fcra). **81 Dorling Kindersley**: (clb); Holts Gems (cla, cra, crb, bc). **82 Dorling Kindersley**: Holts Gems (c, br, bl). **83 Alamy Stock Photo**: Tyrone Siu (br). **Dorling Kindersley**: Holts Gems (cl); Natural History Museum, London (tl, c, cr). **84-85 Alamy Stock Photo**: Martin Siepmann (c). **84 Alamy Stock Photo**: Perry van Munster (c). **85 123RF.com**: Iuliia Grebeniukova (bc). **Alamy Stock Photo**: Charles Marden Fitch (cr). **Dorling Kindersley**: Natural History Museum, London (tl). **86 123RF.com**: Saastaja (cl). **87 Alamy Stock Photo**: WaterFrame_fba (tc). **Dorling Kindersley**: Holts Gems (c); Natural History Museum, London (tr). **88 Dorling Kindersley**: Natural History Museum, London (ca, br, c, cb). **89 Dorling Kindersley**: Natural History Museum, London (cb). **Getty Images**: Hector Mata (tr). **90 123RF.com**: Dipressionist (bc/garnet). **Alamy Stock Photo**: Natural History Museum, London (fcla); Siim Sepp (br). **Dorling Kindersley**: (clb); Holts Gems (cla/Almandin, cl); Natural History Museum, London (cla/Amazonite, ca, bc). **iStockphoto.com**: VvoeVale (cla). **91 Alamy Stock Photo**: Henri Koskinen (crb); RF Company (tr); Phil Degginger / Jack Clark Collection (bc/topaz); Leon Werdinger (clb). **Dorling Kindersley**: Holts Gems (tl); Natural History Museum, London (tc, cla, cl, bc/calcium carbonate, bc/Watermelon Tourmaline, br, cb). **92 Dorling Kindersley**: Holts Gems (cra). **93 Dorling Kindersley**: Natural History Museum, London (bc). **96 Todd Kent, Explorer Multimedia Inc. (Author image) (br)**

Cover images: Front: Dorling Kindersley: Natural History Museum, London cra, cr; **Back: Dorling Kindersley**: Natural History Museum, London tc, bc; **Spine: Dorling Kindersley**: Natural History Museum, London t;
Front Endpapers: Dorling Kindersley: Holts Gems 0ftl, Natural History Museum, London 0tl (Granite), 0tl; **Back Endpapers: Alamy Stock Photo**: Natural History Museum, London 0cr; Dorling Kindersley: 0bc, Holts Gems 0ftl, 0cla (ruby), 0tc (JADEITE GREEN), 0cra, 0crb, 0cla (MOONSTONESMOOTH), Natural History Museum, London 0tl (Granite), 0tl, 0cla, 0crb (moonstone), 0clb, 0cl, 0ca (calcium carbonate rock), 0tl (Uvarovite), 0tc (pencil shaped), 0cr (Crystalline), 0cb (gilson opal), 0cb (Opalescent), 0bc (Amazonite), 0bc (Watermelon Tourmaline).

**All other images © Dorling Kindersley
For further information see:
www.dkimages.com**

About the author

Dr. Devin Dennie is a professional geologist and science communicator based in the USA. He is the writer and presenter of Geology Kitchen, a series of videos explaining geological concepts with food, and other educational television and film on rocks and minerals.